Unbelievable Pictures and Facts About Barcelona

By: Olivia Greenwood

Introduction

Barcelona is known for its art, architecture and sports teams. The city is very popular and there are plenty of things to do and see. Today we will be exploring the interesting city of Barcelona.

Is Barcelona a city which is visited often?

Barcelona is actually the third most visited city in the whole of Europe. Every year millions of people come to visit the city of Barcelona.

Are there many tourist attractions in the city?

There are plenty of wonderful and exciting tourist attractions in Barcelona.

Does Barcelona hold any festivals?

The answer is a big yes. There are all sorts of different festivals which are held in the city.

Does Barcelona celebrate any unique holidays?

Barcelona certainly does celebrate some unique holidays. The most unique one is called the feast of St.Jordis. On this day they celebrate literacy and love. Men give roses to the woman that they love. Women give books to the men they love on this day.

Are there any famous buildings that are still being constructed?

There is a church in Barcelona which goes by the name of La Sagrada Familia. This church was actually designed by the world-famous artist Gaudi. The construction process began in 1882 and it is still busy being built today. It is estimated that it will only be completed in 2026.

Is Barcelona a child-friendly city?

The city is very child-friendly. There are plenty of fun and exciting things for children to do in Barcelona.

Are there any places that are considered to be haunted?

There are some abandoned metro stations in Barcelona which are considered to be haunted. If you believe this or not, it is entirely up to you.

Does Barcelona have many parks?

If you enjoy going to the park, then Barcelona may become your favorite place. There are plenty of magnificent parks all over the city.

Will you find any museums in Barcelona?

If you enjoy museums, then you will love Barcelona. The city is filled with all sorts of fun and interesting museums.

Do many people drive cars in Barcelona?

The answer is a big no. The majority of people in Barcelona make use of public transport. They have a really good public transport system. Driving a car in Barcelona is considered to be very dangerous and there are frequently road accidents taking place.

Will you find any beaches in Barcelona?

Barcelona is known throughout the world for its beaches. There were no beaches in the area until 1991. The beaches were built by the government when Barcelona was selected as the city to host the Olympics in 1992.

Which street in Barcelona has the most people?

The street in Barcelona which sees most people is called Portal de l'Angel. It is estimated that nearly 4 thousand people come through this area every hour.

What sport do people follow the most in Barcelona?

American football is a sport which is followed the most in Barcelona. Not only do they have their own famous football team but they also are home to the biggest stadium in Europe.

What language is spoken in Barcelona?

The people in Barcelona speak two official languages. These languages are Catalan and Spanish.

Which currency do they use in Barcelona?

If you wish to buy things in Barcelona it may be useful for you to know what currency is used. Barcelona makes use of the same currency as the rest of Europe. The currency which they use is the Euro.

What type of landscape is there in Barcelona?

Barcelona has a very attractive landscape. It is surrounded by beautiful mountains and rivers.

What kind of weather will you experience in Barcelona?

The climate in Barcelona can be described as subtropical. During the winter months, the weather is very cold. During the summer months, it can get exceptionally hot.

How many people currently live in Barcelona?

The population in Barcelona is growing each and every year. There are currently over 1.8 million people living in Barcelona.

Is it safe to travel in the city of Barcelona?

The good news is that it is very safe to travel in Barcelona. You should obviously always be careful, but the city itself is an extremely safe place.

Exactly where can Barcelona be found?

If you visit the country of Spain, you will find the city of Barcelona. It is situated on the northeastern side.

Made in the USA
Monee, IL
04 December 2022

19461632R00026